DIGGING UP DINOSAUR FOSSILS IN SOUTH AMERICA

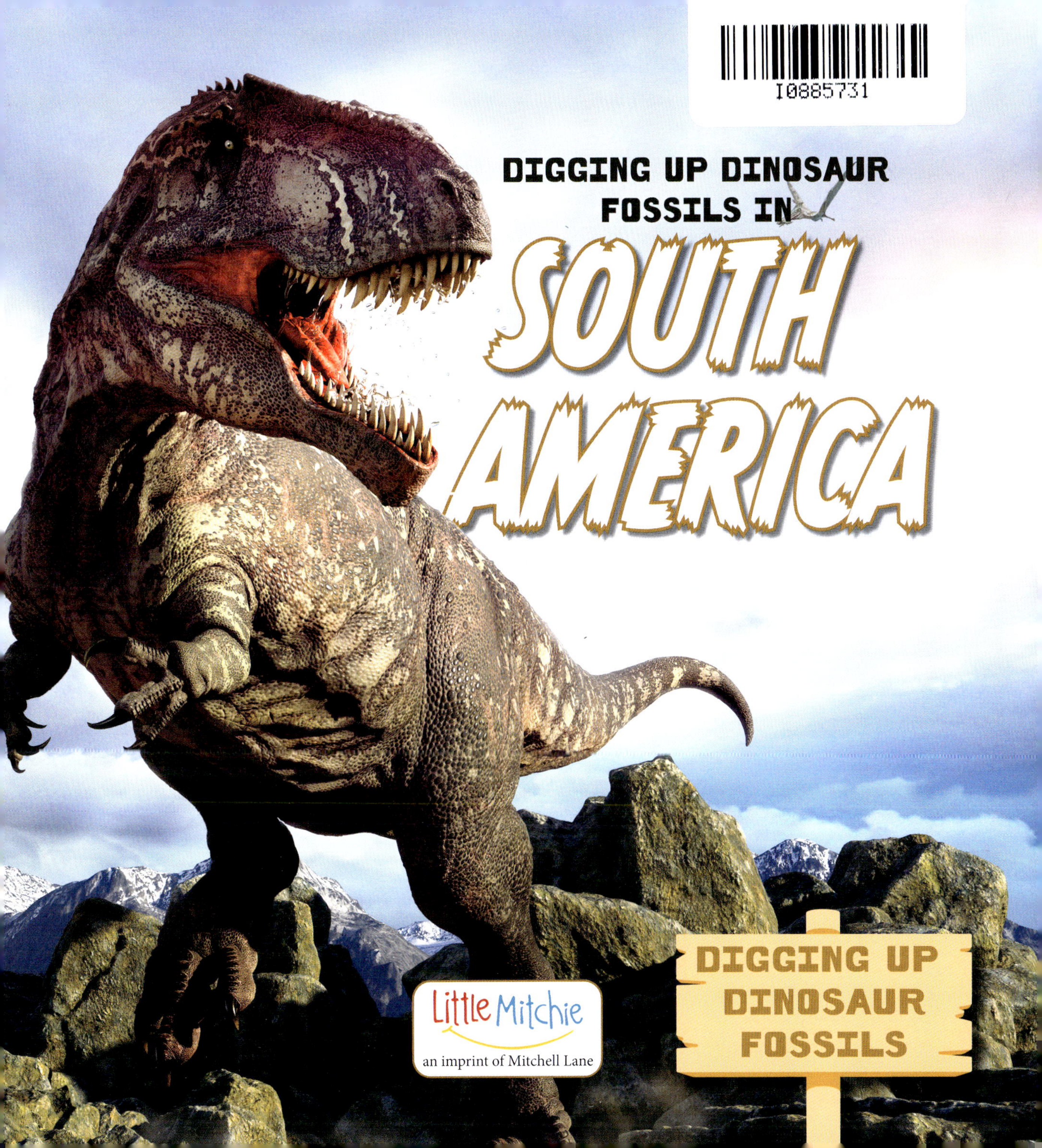

Little Mitchie
an imprint of Mitchell Lane

DIGGING UP DINOSAUR FOSSILS

Creating Young Nonfiction Readers

Little Mitchie lets children delve into nonfiction at beginning reading levels. Young readers are introduced to new concepts, facts, ideas, and vocabulary.

Tips for Reading Nonfiction with Young Readers

Talk about Nonfiction

Begin by explaining that nonfiction books give us information that is true. The book will be organized around a specific topic or idea, and we may learn new facts through reading.

Look at the Parts

Most nonfiction books have helpful features. Our *Little Mitchie* titles include color photographs and graphic aids, a table of contents, a glossary, and an index. Share the purpose of these features with your reader.

Color Photos and Graphic Aids
A lot of information can be found by "reading" photos, charts, maps, and other graphic aids found within nonfiction texts. Help your reader learn more about the different ways information can be displayed.

Table of Contents
Located at the front of the book, this list shows the big ideas within the text and the page numbers where they can be found.

Glossary
Located at the back of the book, the glossary defines key words and phrases that are related to the topic. These words and phrases can be found in the text in colored type.

Index
Located at the back of the book, an index is an alphabetical list of topics and the page numbers where they can be found.

With a little help and guidance about reading nonfiction, you can feel good about introducing a young reader to the world of *Little Mitchie* nonfiction books.

Mitchell Lane
PUBLISHERS

2001 SW 31st Avenue
Hallandale, FL 33009
www.mitchelllanepub.com

Little Mitchie

First Edition, 2025.

Author: Meg Greve
Designer: Rhea Magaro
Editor: Madison Greve

Names/credits:
Title: Digging Up Dinosaur Fossils in South America / by Meg Greve
Description: Hallandale, FL : Mitchell Lane Publishers, [2025]

Series: Digging Up Dinosaur Fossils
Library bound ISBN: 979-8-89260-243-3
Paperback ISBN: 979-8-89260-420-8
eBook ISBN: 979-8-89260-244-0

Little Mitchie is an imprint of Mitchell Lane Publishers.

PHOTO CREDITS
Alamy: Universal Images Group North America LLC/DeAgostini, 8-9, 12-13; Shutterstock: Warpaint, cover, 1, 10-11; Colorcocktail, cover, 1 (sign); Aust28, 4, 6, 9, 11, 13, 15, 17, 18, 20, 23; Catmando, 3; Noiel, 5; Engineer studio, 6-7; Jaroslav Moravcik, 14-15; Herschel Hoffmeyer, 15; Michael Rosskothen, 16-17; Eric Isselee, 19; Elnur, 20-21; Public Domain: 19

CONTENTS

When Dinosaurs Ruled the Land

Volcanoes erupt. Flowers start to grow. The weather is hot and humid. Creatures big and small roam the land eating plants, and eating each other. This was South America before it was a **continent**. This was the time of the dinosaurs!

Before there were seven continents, all land formed one giant continent called Pangea.

Dinosaurs roamed the earth more than 200 million years ago. Paleontologists study their **fossils** to learn about the history of life on our planet. Let's learn about some South American dinosaurs!

DINO DETAILS:
Dinosaurs who walked on two legs could still keep up with smaller, quicker animals.

Meat for Dinner? Meet the Carnivores!

Giganotosaurus is one of the largest dinosaurs ever discovered. It walked on two back legs with two short legs in front. This **predator** ran fast enough to catch the small animals it hunted.

DINO DETAILS:
Dinosaurs who walked on two legs also used their tails for balance.

Eoraptor was one of the first dinosaurs. This **carnivore** was only 1.5 feet (.46 meters) tall. But it was able to hunt animals with its sharp teeth and five sharp claws on each hand. Eoraptor may have eaten plants too!

DINO DETAILS:

Smaller front legs helped dinosaurs grab onto plants or **prey**. They were also used to dig holes for dinosaur eggs.

Piatnitzkysaurus used its large head and strong neck to catch prey. It ate smaller, plant-eating dinosaurs. At times, it would also eat dead animals!

DINO DETAILS:

Dinosaur eggs did not have armor for protection. So dinosaurs hid their eggs in holes covered up with dirt and leaves.

MORE PLANTS FOR THE HERBIVORES, PLEASE!

Saltasaurus had small, bony plates and was one of the first huge **herbivore** fossils found. It had armor built into its body for protection.

DINO DETAILS:
The fossil of the Argentinosaurus shin bone is 5 ft (1.5 m) long!

Argentinosaurus was one of the largest animals to ever walk on Earth. It ate over 882 pounds (400 kilograms) of plants every day. Its neck was about 29 ft (9 m) long. There were air sacs in its neck to keep it from feeling too heavy.

Titanomachya was one of the smallest of the huge herbivores. Even the smallest of this group could reach the size of a minibus!

DINO DETAILS:
Although Titanomachya was the smallest of the huge herbivores, it was about the size of a cow.

Millions of years ago, when South America was just a corner of Pangea, it was home to some of the most interesting dinosaurs to walk the earth. Their fossils can help us understand the world we live in today.

Where Did the Dinosaurs Live?

More than 150 different dinosaur fossils have been found in South America. These are just a few!

- **Giganotosaurus:** Argentina
- **Eoraptor:** northwestern Argentina
- **Piatnitzkysaurus:** Argentina
- **Saltasaurus:** Argentina
- **Argentinosaurus:** Argentina
- **Titanomachya**: Argentina (Patagonia)

Interesting Facts

- The word dinosaur means "terrible lizard."
- Paleontologists can learn a lot about a dinosaur from just one small bone.
- About 66 million years ago, a huge asteroid crashed into Earth that killed off all dinosaurs except for birds.
- Almost all dinosaurs laid their eggs in a nest or small hole.
- Dinosaurs first appeared on Earth about 252 million years ago.

Spotlight On: José Bonaparte

José Bonaparte was a paleontologist from Argentina. As a child, he spent a lot of time outside and began collecting interesting items that he uncovered in the landscape of his hometown. Before he knew it, he had a large collection of dinosaur bones that had never been found before! He discovered more than 25 dinosaurs in South America throughout his life. One of his most well-known discoveries was the Saltasaurus. He inspired many other paleontologists to visit Argentina in search of dinosaur bones. Even as a little boy, Bonaparte discovered some of the biggest living creatures to ever walk this earth.

Glossary

carnivore (KAR-ni-vor):
A meat-eating animal

continent (KON-tin-ent):
One of the seven largest pieces of land on Earth

fossils (FAH-suhls):
Rock that forms after a living thing is preserved in the earth

herbivore (ER-buh-vor):
A plant-eating animal

predator (PRE-duh-ter):
An animal that hunts other animals for food

prey (pray):
Animals hunted and eaten by other animals

Index

Further Reading

Crane, Cody. *All About Fossils: Discovering Dinosaurs and Other Clues to the Past*. New York, NY: Scholastic, 2021.

Johnson-Ransom, Evan. *Dinosaur World*. Nashville, TN: Applesauce Press, 2023.

Stoltz, Susan R. *X-Ray Dinosaurs and Other Prehistoric Creatures*. Phoenix, AZ: Lyric & Stone Publishing, 2022.

On the Internet

Argentinosaurus
https://www.dinopit.com/argentinosaurus
Learn lots of facts about one of the world's largest dinosaurs.

Paleontology: The Big Dig
https://www.amnh.org/explore/ology/paleontology
Learn what it takes to be a paleontologist!